Words of Inspiration for the Worship Leader and Church Musician

SONJA JONES

Love Clones Publishing
www.lcpublishing.net

Printed in the United States of America

First Printing, 2014

ISBN: 978-0692310762

Publishers:
Love Clones Publishing
Chicago, IL 60604
www.lcpublishing.net

DEDICATION

To God, step one is complete! Thank you, Father, for using me.

To my family, I thank God daily for your patience and support as I hear His voice.

To Kingdom Driven Entrepreneur, this is the product of your obedience.

Table of Contents

Introduction

Full circle

"Book? I don't want to learn how to write a book!" God sure does have a sense of humor, doesn't He?

On January 31, 2014 at 1:00pm, I was scheduled to talk to Pastor David Burrus about an assignment he gave me; the task was to study the 12 disciples and find the disciple that best fit my character. I was so excited to tell him what I'd discovered only to have another assignment added to the list. Pastor Burrus double booked my meeting with another member of the group Kingdom Driven Entrepreneur, Tanya Love. She was in the beginning stages of writing a book and Pastor Burrus agreed to teach her how to create a book outline. As I was about to bow out of the conversation gracefully and reschedule, he said (as only Burrus could say it), "you're gonna learn how to write a book today, Doc!" Who am I to pass up free teaching?

The call was fun because the subject that we used to create the outline was praise and worship. The energy of the call was indescribable because the subject of praise and worship is natural to me and to hear it broken down through the outline made me eager to delve deeper into the subject. Every worship leader teaches praise & worship from a different angle. This motivated me to do the unthinkable, well, in my eyes at least.

I asked Pastor Burrus, "Could this outline be used for a devotional?" He agreed, gave me tips for writing a 21 or 30-day devotional and also provided simple modifications to the outline to make it suitable for a devotional. After searching for countless books on praise and worship, it was hard for me to locate a devotional for worship leaders. Never in my mind did I think that God was anointing me for this specific assignment!

As a worship leader and church musician, it is so easy to get caught up in church protocol and miss the voice of God as you carry out your assignment. We have a unique anointing and it must be addressed and protected. I pray that this book will not only strengthen you but also encourage you to share your testimony with other musicians and worship leaders in the Body of Christ. Be encouraged and know that God is faithful to complete the work that He has called you to do.

CHAPTER 1: FOUNDATION

The Passwords of Praise

Ps 89:15a (MSG)- Blessed are the people who know the passwords of praise...

According to dictionary.com, the definition of the word "password" is as follows: "a secret word or phrase that must be used to gain access or approval to something, prove identity, or to keep something secret from those who are not allowed access"

As I read through God's Word and the different translations, I'm always thinking about the translator's reasoning for using certain phrases and words. This chapter was a result of one of those moments. When I read Ps 89:15a, my initial thought was, "Passwords of praise? This would make more sense if it were referring to worship. Why did Eugene Peterson use the word *praise* instead of *worship?*" My second thought was "Why was the word *password* used in the plural tense instead of the singular tense?" As I began to study this passage, I was in awe of God's use of Brother Peterson; the revelation he received blew my mind! So let me break this down:

The first definition of a password is that it's *a secret word or phrase that must be used to gain access or approval to something*. All of us have different passwords for access to different types of information, from our email account to our bank account. Depending on the type of account we're trying to setup, the password that we select will be strong or weak. It's recommended that we have strong passwords for information that's more valuable to us; the stronger the password, the better it protects you from unauthorized access. Also, strong passwords are not easily identifiable. Your stronger passwords may not have your initials, nickname, or names of your family members. They may have special characters, capitalized letters, numbers, or a combination of all three.

Our relationship with God is like a password. Depending on how valuable it is to us, it can be strong or weak in God's eyes. If our relationship with God is weak, resembling the values of the world, it's undesirable and no one has an interest in knowing about it. If our relationship with God is strong, our light will pique the curiosity of unbelievers, creating value to this unexplainable attraction to our Father, how He operates, and why we follow Him. When we enter into the presence of God, the highest level of access, the relationship is so unique and intimate that it can only be shared between you and Him. Our desire is to check the strength of our password daily, knowing that, as time progresses, our password will change and reflect the level of access we have to God.

The second definition of a password is that it *proves identity*. It's advised that you avoid using the same password for every account that you own because it increases the chances of someone compromising your identity. As you compare your life before you met Christ to your current relationship with Christ, it would be difficult for you to make these two life phases similar because a relationship with God requires transformation. You are not the same person you were before you met Christ and that's the way it should be. A life of worship guarantees change. Regarding our spiritual password, it should reflect our current account (season of life), and should not have any remnants of our former accounts. God wants us to start communicating with Him in ways unrelated to man's standard of logic. God is looking for people who are hungry for Him outside of church, desire to seek His face daily through the reading and application of His Word, and are willing to fast and pray under the unction of the Holy Spirit. Our constant curiosity for God will get His attention and, like a password, will authenticate us as God-chasers and allow us access to His presence.

The third definition of a password is that it *keeps something secret from those who are not allowed access*. Creating unique passwords will not only give us greater access to God but will also prevent unauthorized access from the enemy. For my retirement account, it's a requirement for me to change my password annually and my password cannot resemble any of my previous passwords. As we grow in God, our passwords will become more unique, representing the current level or season of our walk with Him. Each new level will require a new password and each password will be more distinctive, and stronger, than the previous one. Glory to God!

God is saying to us, "if you want full access to Me, no one else can have access to your password!" What is your current password? As you reflect on the previous seasons in your life, how has your password changed? Can you make a declaration of your future passwords? In the next chapter, I will share with you how your password has an affect on your interpretation of the terms praise and worship.

The Difference between Praise and Worship

Jeremiah 29:13-14a (MSG) - "When you come looking for me, you'll find me. "Yes, when you get serious about finding me and want it more than anything else, I'll make sure you won't be disappointed." God's Decree.

When I began my walk with Christ, I thought that the two words, praise and worship, were the same. We praise God at church; we also worship Him at church. As I began playing for churches and participating in the choir, I started to see these words differently. Praise is loud; worship is quiet. Praise songs are upbeat; worship songs are slower in tempo. Praise is shouting, running, and hollering. Worship is crying and/or lifting your hands. Now, as I enter my mid-thirties, I'm truly beginning to understand the difference between praise and worship.

In the blog *worshipministry.com*, Gary Miller shares others' interpretations of these words. Below are some of the ones that I found interesting:

- Praise is lifting up; worship is bowing down.
- Praise is for what God has done; worship is for who God is.

- Praise is “the opening”; worship is “the entering”.
- Praise is always visible; worship has the option of being visible.
- Praise can be done from afar; worship must be done in His presence.
- To praise God means we call Him to our presence; to worship God means He calls us to His presence.

The more I read these, it motivated me to search my heart for what praise and worship meant to me. Here are some of my interpretations:

- Praise is acknowledging God in the moment; worship is acknowledging God in our lifestyle.
- Praise is like rolling out the red carpet; worship is going through the threshold of the big event.
- When I praise, I say, “God is great” (I describe Him); when I worship, I say, “God is worthy” (I value Him).
- Praise is the vehicle to the holy place; worship is dwelling there.
- Praise is talking about God; worship is talking to God.
- Praise is fellowship with God; worship is relationship with God.
- Praise is community; worship is intimacy.
- Praise is one day (temporary); worship is everyday (permanent).

- Praise is a verb; worship is a noun.
- Praise is to know of God; worship is to know God.
- We praise God through our words; we worship God in our actions.
- When I praise God, I speak of Him; when I worship God, I seek Him.

If you notice, none of these comparisons are exactly the same. As you actively seek God's face, you will be able to define praise and worship as it relates to you. This makes perfect sense because every person's relationship with God is unique; none of us will experience God in the exact same way. I encourage you to take advantage of your smartphone's memo app, your Bible app, your sound recorder, or a memo pad and jot down the experiences and revelations God gives you. You will be amazed at the number of times God speaks to you and also *how* He speaks to you. Stay focused and stay seeking Him!

The Quiet Place

1 Kings 19:11-13 (NCV) -The Lord said to Elijah, "Go, stand in front of me on the mountain, and I will pass by you." Then a very strong wind blew until it caused the mountains to fall apart and large rocks to break in front of the Lord. But the Lord was not in the wind. After the wind, there was an earthquake, but the Lord was not in the earthquake. After the earthquake, there was a fire, but the Lord was not in the fire. After the fire, there was a quiet, gentle sound. When Elijah heard it, he covered his face with his coat and went out and stood at the entrance to the cave. Then a voice said to him, "Elijah! Why are you here?"

In his sermon, "Worship to Go," Israel Haughton described one of his moments as a beginning worship leader. There was a particular parishioner, whom he called Suzie Sandpaper that had something to say after every worship service; as you can imagine, she irritated Israel to no end. One Sunday, Ms. Sandpaper surprisingly gave Israel some advice instead of her usual criticism. She suggested that he go home and spend some quiet, intimate time with God.

That evening, Israel moved his piano into the kitchen, sat some small objects on top of the piano to act as his audience, and played. Once he began to play, the Lord gave him lyrics and soon God's presence saturated his apartment. It was through that experience that Israel understood the essence of worship - intimacy.

According to Webster's Dictionary, the definition of intimacy is:

- A close, familiar, and usually affectionate or loving personal relationship with another person or group.
- A close association with or detailed knowledge or deep understanding of a place, subject, or period of history

Think about it, most of your intimate relationship encounters are in places where it's just you and that person. Although you may be in a public place, the opportunity to spend time with that person is intentional and valuable because you understand that the time spent with them strengthens your relationship. We don't spend time with anyone or anything that doesn't add value to our lives.

Since God desires intimate relationships with His creation, His communication with us is the most effective in the environments where He has our full attention. For me, that environment is my car, my shower, or in my office (where the piano is). God will speak to you in a still, small voice because He wants to be as close to you as possible. The more time you spend with God, the clearer His voice will be! It's in these times where He will give you specific instructions on how to lead His people into His presence.

My advice to you is to spend one day in complete silence and talk to Him throughout the day as if He was hanging out with you. Avoid the TV, radio, phone, or anything that would distract you. You'll be amazed at how clear God's voice becomes. If you seek God diligently, scripture says that He will reward you (Heb. 11:6). Make it a habit to be quiet with God; He will reward you with revelation that will free the spiritually captive and draw them to His saving grace.

CHAPTER 2: IDENTITY

I Was Created to Worship God

*"When you're clothed with God's **blessing**, there is no way you can remain **average** or **common**. God's **glory** will cause you to rise far above **statistics** and **stereotypes**. You're not like everybody else. You're **different**, that's why you can make a **difference**."* ~ Billie Miller, "The Motivational Minister"

Jeremiah 1:5 (NCV) - Before I made you in your mother's womb, I chose you. Before you were born, I set you apart for a special work. I appointed you as a prophet to the nations.

Isn't it amazing to know that God had YOU in mind when he was seeking people that would make His name great in the earth?

Think back to the first time you took interest in singing or playing an instrument. For me, I remember receiving my first keyboard at 6 years old. Once I began taking piano lessons, I also remember writing the melody to the song "Spread My Wings" by R&B group Troop. In 4th grade, my goal was to be the next Spinderella and my mama almost killed me for tearing up the needle on her

Emerson turntable stereo. I participated in the band from 7th-12th grade, was blessed with an opportunity to sing at Carnegie Hall my senior year of high school with our gospel choir, and later received a bachelor's degree in Music Education. After college, I taught elementary music for 12 years while serving as a church musician and also teaching private piano lessons. I never thought that those events would lead me to where I am now.

All of the various phases in your life have led you to this moment in your journey. Don't forget to thank God for those precious moments; He will reveal the relevance of those specific events as you progress.

Throughout your journey, you will meet other musicians and singers with different gifts. Don't fall into the enemy's trap of comparing yourself to others. Although we don't share the same experiences does not mean that we don't share the same purpose. Every worship leader has the responsibility of ushering God's people into the presence of God. Many of us are anointed to work with the youth, write songs of faith and redemption, or change the hearts of nations. If you don't know the specifics of your calling, don't worry; God will reveal it to you in His perfect timing. Always be prepared to minister by studying the Word, praying, fasting, and improving your gift on a continual basis.

Read Esther 4:14 and 2 Tim 2:15 (NCV) and remember.... YOU are ANNOINTED for this!

Acknowledging who I am as a worship leader

Romans 11:29 (NCV)- God never changes his mind about the people he calls and the things he gives them.

There are thousands of worship leaders, church musicians, psalmists, ministers of music, but there is only one YOU! You have been chosen by God to communicate His love to the masses through song.

When God graced you with this gift, it was on purpose. The best part about this verse is that this gift remains in you regardless of how you perform. God doesn't love us based on our performance; imagine where we'd be if that *was* the case! There would be no reason for Jesus to die; it would truly have been a lost cause from day one.

You have been anointed by God to complete this assignment. You may not feel adequate because of the leaders who were in place before you or your fellow laborers that are more skilled than you. Don't be concerned about that! In Samuel 16, God chose David, through the prophet Samuel, to be King of Israel. The cool part about it was that he was chosen from among his brothers who had more experience in leadership. Allow God to use you in your current stage of development;

for each level of your assignment, He has a specific lesson for you to learn. Prophecies do not happen overnight; they lay the foundation for God's plan and glory to be revealed in you. If you love God, serve Him, and be amazed at what He does through your YES!

Don't Compare Yourself to Others: The Spirit of Comparison

2 Corinthians 10:4-5 (NCV) -We fight with weapons that are different from those the world uses. Our weapons have power from God that can destroy the enemy's strong places. We destroy people's arguments and every proud thing that raises itself against the knowledge of God. We capture every thought and make it give up and obey Christ.

Jeremiah 1:5-8 (NLT) -"I knew you before I formed you in your mother's womb. Before you were born I set you apart and appointed you as my prophet to the nations." "O Sovereign Lord," I said, "I can't speak for you! I'm too young!" The Lord replied, "Don't say, 'I'm too young,' for you must go wherever I send you and say whatever I tell you. And don't be afraid of the people, for I will be with you and will protect you. I, the Lord, have spoken!"

My second music ministry assignment was a long one. I served as a pianist from 2003-2011 and as minister of music from 2011-2012. When our minister of music moved to North Carolina, he gave me an encouraging word and I felt confident that the choir would continue to minister as if he never left. To my amazement, the choir took a full turn in the opposite direction. I took full responsibility for the choir's downfall and resigned after a year in the position. I felt like a complete failure and vowed never to lead another choir for a long time.

Several questions ran through my mind during my difficulties with the choir and after my resignation. How could I be effective teaching worship at the private school and not be effective teaching the church choir? Another question was, why didn't the choir and musicians continue with the same standard of excellence as our former minister of music taught us? I would beat myself up every week by hearing church members say, "The choir will never be as good as…", "You don't play, sing, or direct like…", and "The choir will never respect you because you're not…". God never gave me specific answers to these questions, but He did reveal something to me- my experiences, positive or negative, will prepare and strengthen me for His call on my life.

There are thousands of church musicians, worship leaders, psalmists, etc., but there will only be one Sonja Jones. God has given me a specific anointing and He will allow it to be used in specific places at specific times. Sometimes, as worship leaders, we try to follow salary, convenience, and status. When we do this, we tune out God's voice and run the risk of being ineffective. We can't hear God's voice unless we communicate with Him daily. The way to receive discernment and peace about our assignments is through prayer and knowledge of Scripture.

If you feel yourself getting discouraged, rest in the promise that God has a plan for your life. Give all of those insecurities to God. The Bible says that He will give you power to capture those thoughts and force them to obey His word. Don't allow yourself to become ineffective another day due to negative thinking. You have a job to do!

You Are Anointed to Bless Others

Matthew 27: 27-54 (NLT)- The Roman officer and the other soldiers at the crucifixion were terrified by the earthquake and all that had happened. They said, "This man truly was the Son of God!"

Every person on earth has a God-ordained assignment. Yes, that includes you! Believe it or not, you are the answer to someone's problem. As a worship leader, the answer to someone's life situation may come through the songs that you sing. We're not talking about hitting the right notes, mastering the lyrics from memory, or even selecting the right songs; God has empowered you to deliver those songs through a unique tool called *transparency*. In other words, people should see God straight through your personal challenges and victories.

Many of us have heard the story of Jesus' crucifixion, but not from the perspective of the centurion (Matthew 27: 27-54 NLT). As many of us, the centurion was going through the motions of life. Although he may have questioned Jesus' innocence throughout the process (Scripture doesn't say exactly), I'm sure that he participated in the mockery and said some unkind things, you know, following the crowd. However, once he saw the sky become dark, the rocks split, and the dead rise, the centurion knew that what he was experiencing was something far beyond natural circumstance. He was experiencing a move of God. For God to have moved in the way that He did, Jesus had to surrender himself completely. Think about it. Jesus had been beaten, spat on, mocked, nailed to a cross, given vinegar to drink, stabbed, and eventually gave His life to the Father. All of these actions were necessary for God to move to the point of acknowledgement from the centurion. Once the presence of God was evident, the centurion humbled himself and worshipped.

Many worship leaders do not fully comprehend the importance of transparency when ushering people into the presence of God. This doesn't mean to expose *all* of your business to your fellow parishioners. Your relationship with God is evident in your worship, and, as we teach our choirs the motto "you perform how you practice," you will usher people into the knowledge of God that you're currently experiencing. Depending on your relationship and knowledge of God, you can be leading the sheep beside quiet waters, pushing the sheep in the water, or leaving them alone to die (Psalm 23)! Do you know God? How has He transformed your life? How has He changed your family members or your friends? What Bible verses have made you more aware of God's power? Use these experiences to share with others the God whom you love and serve. Be a filter!

Chapter 3: My Current Assignment

My Job is a Divine Assignment

Romans 8:28 (AMP)- We are assured and know that [God being a partner in their labor] all things work together and are [fitting into a plan] for good to and for those who love God and are called according to [His] design and purpose.

As many of you are reading this devotional, I've played at different churches, lead workshops, and sang. I've also taught elementary music and private piano, flute, and voice lessons. Some of those assignments were great experiences, others, not so much. As God has strengthened me through every experience, I do not regret any part of my journey.

In every assignment God gives you, make it a priority to learn from it. He'll reveal to you new strategies, techniques, resources, and also expose your faults. Thank God for the newness in your assignments and take full advantage of them. Thank God also for the "thorns in your flesh"; your faults justify your need for Him daily.

As you're laboring in your current assignment, ask God to reveal to you the mission. Stay yielded and wake up daily in full expectation of a fresh lesson. Feel free to journal your experiences; what you endure today will bless another worship leader in his or her path. Remember that every assignment is necessary to prepare you for your purpose!

Serving your church

Psalm 90:17 (GNT)- Lord our God, may your blessings be with us. Give us success in all we do!

There's nothing greater than a musician who is punctual, great at communicating with church leadership, prepared, and has a servant's heart. You can't say that you love God and don't have a heart of service. Period. As well, if you're walking in purpose, you will give nothing less than excellence to God. God likes good stuff too!

I've been in churches where I've witnessed musicians listening to the songs for the first time at the rehearsal before Sunday service; the choir was more prepared than the musician! This is not a proper example of stewardship when the musician is receiving a salary for zero effort while the choir is making a sacrificial offering of their time and effort with no monetary compensation. Don't be that person; God never operates in disorder. The ministry will always be as fruitful as its leader.

To serve God in excellence, you must have a sacrificial mindset (2 Samuel 24:24). Taking time out of your busy schedule to ensure that your choir is prepared, to check on members of your choir when they haven't been to church in a while, and meeting the requests of your pastor are examples of the tasks in your assignment. Yes, you may have to handle these tasks during inconvenient times, but you must keep in mind that your reward won't be seen on earth. To edify God's kingdom means to serve the way God expects you to serve.

Staying in your Lane

1 Samuel 16:19 (NIV) - Then Saul sent messengers to Jesse and said, "Send me your son David, who is with the sheep."

As I'm writing this book, I am currently serving at my home church as a choir member. I also assist with the children's choir. Guess what? I'm totally fine with that!

I've been a church musician and an elementary music teacher since 2001; as I served in different churches, I was always placed in a music ministry or a children's ministry because of my expertise. There were many times I wanted to say, "I'm gifted in other areas besides music and children's ministry," but it was difficult to find people to assist me so I could explore other talents. Being good at something can be both a blessing and a curse. Although you want to thrive and excel in the things you're good at, sometimes those shiny compliments overshadow your opportunity to experience other gifts. That other gift for me was being a worship leader.

After David was anointed to be king in I Samuel 16, he did not have a fancy coronation. He remained at his father's home and continued to herd sheep. In the series *Sticks and Stones*, Pastor Steven Furtick gives us insight into this phase of

David's life. Although David was anointed to be king, his current assignment didn't change. We assume that when a person receives a new job that it's a symbol of a greater anointing. God will give you a fresh revelation, awareness, and anointing in your current assignment. What sets you apart is your action after the revelation. If you're operating under a greater anointing, your actions should be different, regardless of your position or location.

Knowing your purpose will allow you to one, be content where God leads you and two, be an effective servant. You're not concerned about the activity of others nor do you have time to be! You have a clear understanding of what you can and can't do. Since I was a musician and was aware of my responsibility to the church where I served, I couldn't disrespect the vision of the pastor and those co-laboring with me by doing what I wanted to do.

When God was ready to shift me, it wasn't overnight; he placed me in a period of preparation. I had a unique experience with Him in January 2014 that confirmed the calling of worship on my life and since then God has sent mentors, teachers, and co-laborers in the worship ministry to pour wisdom into me. Don't you know that God also gave me a mentee for me to pour into during my preparation time? This young lady was preparing for what I was coming out of, as the preachers would say, "you'll catch that on your way home." God loves you so much that He prepares you before He places you on the platform. Allow Him to groom you! Just like we hide our valuables before we leave the house, God hides you, His valuable one, before He shares you with the world. Be diligent in your current assignment, stay yielded, and allow God to prepare your heart for greater!

Serving with Excellence

Mark 12:30 (NLT)-And you must love the Lord your God with all your heart, all your soul, all your mind, and all your strength.

In August 2013, our house was experiencing financial transition; we were a one-income household. A music ministry opportunity that I applied for months before became available. Although my husband enjoyed us attending church as a family, I couldn't just sit and allow our financial status to plunder. We decided to talk with our pastor about the assignment and he gave me the blessing to accept the job. He encouraged me to serve diligently because I'll never know what opportunities may arise from this assignment.

During my ministry assignment, God taught me the importance of following Him and not the money. Although the pay was good, the choir director was spirit-led, and the parishioners were extremely loving, I didn't have any peace. For the first time in a long time, my assignment felt like a job. God didn't send me there; I accepted the job because our house needed a financial boost. Nevertheless, I gave it my best as I served because that's what God required of me. As a result, when it was time for me to leave, I was given an invitation to come back.

Our attitudes and actions will reveal how much we truly love God. Even when we place ourselves in situations where God didn't lead us, God will provide opportunities of deliverance if we repent and choose to follow His lead. (I Corinthians 10:13).

Chapter 4: Skill/Talent

What's the Difference

1 Samuel 16:18 (NLT)- One of the servants said to Saul, "One of Jesse's sons from Bethlehem is a talented harp player. Not only that—he is a brave warrior, a man of war, and has good judgment. He is also a fine-looking young man, and the Lord is with him".

"The separation of talent and skill is one of the greatest misunderstood concepts for people who are trying to excel, who have dreams, who want to do things. Talent you have naturally. Skill is only developed by hours and hours and hours of beating on your craft." - Will Smith

I am a talented singer, but my talents created opportunities for me to develop new skills. When it comes to presenting our talents to God, Pastor Steven Furtick of Elevation Church said it best: "God likes good stuff!"

Most of us, as worship leaders, have had someone tell us how "talented" we are in our singing, playing, or songwriting. As we travel along our journey, we soon realize that we can't be influential on talent alone. Talent that's nurtured and developed is what we call *skill.* If we're God-seekers, it should be our desire to give God our personal best at all times. How do we develop our talents? Matt. 6:33 gives us a good start. Seek God through prayer and fasting. Ask Him to reveal to you His plan for your talent and the resources to develop it.

When David was referred to play for King Saul, he was known for his talent before he was noticed as a follower of God. If you're currently developing your skill in a secular environment, be prepared to be used. God will use your talent to compel others to Christ, especially those who may not experience Him in a traditional worship environment. Just like the interaction of Jesus and the woman at the well, God constantly seeks the hearts of willing souls that are longing for eternal change. Guess what? You may be the vessel that He uses! Your developed talent is the fishing rod that brings in the fish. Are you ready to cast your line? Will your bait attract any fish?

Developing your skill

1 Corinthians 15:30-31 (MSG) -And why do you think I keep risking my neck in this dangerous work? I look death in the face practically every day I live. Do you think I'd do this if I wasn't convinced of your resurrection and mine as guaranteed by the resurrected Messiah Jesus?

The people I've grown to admire are those who purposely look for something new to learn everyday. The movie *The Bucket List* inspired me to literally learn until I die. As Kingdom servants, we should possess that same fervor when it comes to our assignment; we should never stop desiring to learn something new about God and His plan for our lives. Google's definition of development is *to grow or cause to grow and become more mature, advanced, or elaborate.* Your desire to develop your God-breathed skill will reveal your maturity, elevate you into higher realms of the Spirit, and lead you to affirm others in their assignments.

What does skill development look like for the worship leader and musician? First, you have to chase God with everything you've got! He desires an authentic relationship with you; talk to Him like you talk to your friends. Fellowship with Him through prayer and fasting. Intercede for others.

Give your resources! Second, step outside of your church and see what God is doing around you. I began my music ministry in a Missionary Baptist Church and I stuck with that for the majority of my years of service. However, I've learned a lot about worship through other denominations, listening to contemporary Christian radio stations, and subscribing to different worship leaders' podcasts and YouTube channels. Don't keep God in your comfortable box; He wants to reveal things to you in other environments.

As we "die" daily, we learn daily! As we yield to God, we tell Him "I want to learn what YOU want me to learn." Prepare yourself to reflect on every experience, good and bad. Are you hungry for God? Do you desire His heart or what's in His hand? Discipleship is risky in the world's eyes, but you must work from a spiritual perspective. Your ultimate reward is eternity with our Father!

Trusting the Process

Isaiah 40: 29-31 (MSG) -He energizes those who get tired, gives fresh strength to dropouts. For even young people tire and drop out, young folk in their prime stumble and fall. But those who wait upon God get fresh strength. They spread their wings and soar like eagles. They run and don't get tired, they walk and don't lag behind.

Everyone has a "how I got started" story and many of us laugh as we tell the story because that's where we WERE! Many of you will agree that those moments weren't as comical when we were going through them, but it's a testimony of God's grace in our lives.

Throughout our journey, we've all had experiences that have embarrassed us, but we've grown from those hard and hurtful places. Those small beginnings have shaped us into the disciples we are today. I wished on several occasions that God would download organ techniques into me as I slept, but I'm glad that God doesn't operate that way. He's not a genie. Because of this, I still sound like a pianist on the organ. I'll get it together one day.

For those of you who are new to worship ministry, be encouraged to know that you won't get it right most of the time. Be open to accept criticism; everything that sounds and looks good isn't good for you or your ministry. Be confident in your current skill level; you may not have the *chops* to play the flashy intro, but use another portion of the song as your intro or create an intro that doesn't take away from the essence of the song. You will want to give up, but remember that ministry isn't designed to be a place of comfort; it's a place of sacrifice (Luke 9:23 KJV).

To the seasoned ministers of music, as God will give us leaders to develop. They will always come eager to participate in ministry, very similar to a person willing to jump off of a cliff with a running start. Our past experiences are like parachutes to future leaders; He uses them to not only strengthen us but to empower others to jump in with their eyes wide open, reducing the risk of a fatal fall. Always be honest; tell the truth in love. Pray for discernment as you release assignments to your leaders in training. Accept the lesson that God is teaching YOU in this season of leadership. Lastly, be accessible.

We are the eagles that Isaiah refers to in this passage; we've waited on God to develop us and now we are soaring. We haven't "made it" by any means, but we are in a place in our ministries to strengthen the downtrodden. Remember that there are young eagles looking at us from below. Don't poop on them.

Boundaries - I'm more than my skill

Mark 6:30-31 (NIV) -The apostles gathered around Jesus and reported to him all they had done and taught. Then, because so many people were coming and going that they did not even have a chance to eat, he said to them, "Come with me by yourselves to a quiet place and get some rest."

Throughout most of my music ministry, I was a single parent. In addition, I worked three jobs, a full-time music teacher, a church musician, and I taught private piano lessons. My boys and I spent more time in my car than in the house. When we were in the house, somebody was always there until a few before bedtime. I rarely spent quality time with my children. I rarely went on trips and vacations due to my numerous obligations.

My biggest regret to this day was missing my oldest son's 5th grade football career. One of my neighbors would give me the commentary of how he made his first touchdown, his first tackle, and interceptions. I was at home teaching piano lessons so I could pay bills. My son never complained, but I knew that he was disappointed. After that season, I vowed to never miss another game. God answered my prayer, but it wasn't in the way I thought He'd answer it.

In Matthew 6:7, Jesus sends the disciples in pairs to minister in various areas and he gives them specific instructions. Once the disciples return in verse 30, they sit with Jesus and discuss the details of their assignments. As they were talking with Jesus, people were coming from everywhere to see Him. If you can imagine, this was quite a distraction and possibly left the disciples frustrated. Think about it, they had just returned from ministry, they had to report back to Jesus and sit and listen to the other 11 talk about their experiences, plus they had to attend to the growing crowd forming around them. They were so busy that they didn't get a chance to eat. Recognizing the sacrifice of the disciples, Jesus affirmed them by advising them to rest.

In 2012, God was preparing me for a big shift in my life that I was completely unaware of. During my son's football career, I was engaged and my fiancé's biggest fear was that my busy schedule would affect my health. Once we married in 2013, God began to rearrange my private lesson schedule, and I stepped away from my ministerial assignment to be a member of my husband's church. In 2014, my father unexpectedly had heart surgery, which led to the closing of our real estate business. At the same time, I was hired to become the operations manager of a new charter school, which resulted in the closing of my piano studio. I am currently working one full-time job and that's it. Does it feel weird? Of course it does, but I understand that God is calling me to a place of rest. Without this rest, I couldn't receive God's instruction for my next assignment. Guess what that assignment was?

As a musician, it's hard to step away from your instrument. You not only have to play on Sunday, you have to prepare for rehearsal, and you're on call for funerals, revivals, and other impromptu events. Creating purposeful time away from church is necessary because, if you're like me, you can't hear God's still, small voice in your busy life. God is pleased when His servants rest! He longs for those intimate moments with you. Take time to go to an unfamiliar place, sit and be filled! I pray that you have the relationship with your pastor to do so. If not, ask God for strategy on how to present this to your spiritual leader. You are important to God and He needs you whole and healthy to edify His kingdom.

Growing with your Church

Joshua 3:5 (NIV) - Joshua told the people, "Consecrate yourselves, for tomorrow the Lord will do amazing things among you."

One of the most admirable character traits of a person is their ability to grow from weakness. Making a decision to improve a weakness reveals a person's selflessness. The person understands that the gifts God has given them are to be used to edify others.

Joshua is about to take on a mighty feat in Joshua chapter 3. I wonder what his thoughts were as he prepared the Israelites to cross the Jordan? In Joshua 1, he was installed as the new leader of the Israelites after Moses died. He was terrified! God encouraged Joshua to go forth in his new assignment because He promised to be with him. I'm pretty sure that Joshua had some moments of reflection between chapters 1 and 3. Joshua knew that the mission could not be accomplished if he continued to walk in fear; therefore, he had to make some character adjustments and talk with his Leader on a frequent basis. Throughout his leadership journey, Joshua had to use the lessons of his former battles and the voice of his Leader to strengthen him for his future assignments.

As a servant in music ministry, the most destructive thing that you can do is to be complacent! Your ministry is more than your position on the church program (aka 'the A and B selection'). Desire to learn new things. Being bored at church is a red flag!

Do you know the pastor's vision for the church? If not, schedule a meeting ASAP! Your role is to assist in setting the atmosphere so the congregation can receive God's Word. Ask your pastor how the music ministry can enhance the vision of the church.

If you're ready for God to do a new thing in you, commit to spending time with Him; the more you desire to fellowship with God, He will reveal His desires for you and everything you put your hand to! As you seek God's face, reflect on your music ministry's service in the past year. How have you grown? What was awesome and why did you think it was awesome? What could have been better? Why didn't it work and provide a solution? Did certain things happen that you didn't understand-either in the music ministry or outside of the ministry? These questions will help take you and your church to a new level in ministry.

Your Gift Will Make Room

Proverbs 18:16 (VOICE)- The right gift at the right time can open up new opportunities and gains access to influential people.

As it relates to my ministry in worship I am indebted to three awesome ladies, Mrs. Joan Scott, Ms. Briddie Douglas and Dr. Nicole Robinson. They saw something in me that had not been revealed to me yet. Ms. Briddie and Ms. Joan encouraged me to play for the St. Paul youth choir and Dr. Robinson recommended me for my first music teaching position at a local private school. From my teaching position, I established a friendship with my principal, Mr. Tom Benton. After my principal resigned, he was called to open a charter school. A year before the school opened, he asked me to be a part of his school's administrative team. Although I didn't have a clue as to what I was doing back then, these individuals saw potential in me and encouraged me to grow in my gift.

One of the best Bible studies I ever participated in was with Pastor David Burrus in January 2014. Before the Kingdom Driven Entrepreneur Retreat, he encouraged me to study the disciples, select the one that best represented me, and explain why. As I worked on my assignment, it was so interesting to see that every disciple had a specific purpose in Jesus' ministry. The coolest part of this assignment was that Jesus didn't assign their ministerial roles based on the disciples' previous occupations. Jesus used their obedience to Him in their natural assignments to prepare them for their spiritual assignments. Their obedience to God was the foundation of their influence.

Many of us take Proverbs 18:16 as "your gift will give you riches". Although provision is promised as we follow God's will, we can't forget the influence God also provides as we yield ourselves to Him. How you shine your light will either draw others to Christ or make Him undesirable.

People will notice your grace when you are serving obediently to God. When you accept God's call for your life, He will send individuals that will pour into you spiritually. Just as someone saw God's grace in you, you have a responsibility to pour into others once you see their grace. Pray and ask God for guidance on how to lead effectively.

Chapter 5: Transition

Assignments are Temporary

1 Kings 17:5-7 (NCV) - So Elijah did what the Lord said; he went to Kerith Ravine, east of the Jordan, and lived there. The birds brought Elijah bread and meat every morning and evening, and he drank water from the stream. After a while the stream dried up because there was no rain.

Elijah was a prophet of the Lord and served God diligently. Elijah's ministry was so powerful because He was obedient to God and did everything God told him to do. Elijah understood God was not limited to time and space therefore, he could not be concerned about time and space either.

As a worship leader, there are specific reasons why we decide to move to different assignments. Maybe you're not receiving the support of the pastor or the pay may not be suitable for your current lifestyle. Have you ever left an assignment for a logical reason, only to realize that you made a mistake? I have and I'm here to tell you that God taught me a valuable lesson about doing what I wanted to do versus doing what He's instructed me to do.

Like the seasons, God will direct our steps and lead us to various assignments. Some will last longer than others; however, we must be so in tune with God's voice that we're prepared to move when He calls us to do so. We can't be concerned with who we're going to disappoint, how much money we're going to make, or the location or our next assignment.

As you're obeying the voice of God and preparing for transition in your assignment, don't allow your desires (i.e. money, pride) to direct your purpose. If you're walking in God's will, provision will be established; it's nothing to even think about! God will take care of all of your needs, both physical and spiritual. God will never lead you to an assignment where you're not fruitful. Following the voice of God brings peace in every situation. If you're presented an opportunity and there's no peace about it, that's not an assignment from God. Ask God for discernment daily so you can hear Him clearly when it pertains to the appropriate assignments for your purpose. Move forward and be ready to serve wherever God sends you!

Trusting God's Timing

Matthew 28:20b (VOICE)- And I will be with you, day after day, to the end of the age.

I'm learning that those God moments are the ones that are easiest to remember. …

I was at TGI Friday's with two good friends August 2012. My family's property management company was enduring a good run of exposure. In 2011, we wanted to meet the needs of non-profit organizations that couldn't find adequate housing by connecting them to neighborhood landlords who were willing to give their clients "second-chance" housing; many of these families had poor credit and had experienced recent evictions. We were very successful in assisting these organizations, to the extent that the need exceeded the supply.

It was a humbling experience. In addition, I'd recently became engaged, which was a miracle in and of itself. I was totally fine being a single parent (aka I can do bad all by myself, Ms. I-N-D-E-P-E-N-D-E-N-T, etc.), but God was showing me how to be receptive to His plan. Months after surrendering my relationships to God, He blessed me with someone who loved Him more than he loved me.

As I sat with my friends, I confidently said aloud, "this will be my last year at the school". A few seconds later, after I realized what I'd said, I panicked on the inside. Our property management company wasn't making enough money for me to leave my full-time job. I also taught piano lessons and played for a local church, but that income was cushion for the property management business, in case something unexpected happened. I truly didn't see how God would make this happen. Little did I know that it takes circumstances like these to really see God the Teacher.

During the school year, the thought of me leaving became less stressful and more peaceful. I made a vision board with my final date of employment and wrote other motivational acronyms and Bible verses that encouraged me throughout my journey. God also instructed me to save a portion of my earnings to assist with bills during the summertime. Issues at school that would've upset me didn't phase me; it felt as if I was surrounded by an impenetrable force field, protecting me from unnecessary drama. When the time came for me to resign, I had the opportunity to take a few days to pray and talk with my husband, but I didn't need to because God had instructed me and my husband gave me his blessing as well.

Now, I can't end the story saying that everything was a bed of roses. As a matter of fact, summer 2013 was everything but pleasant. Our home was emotionally and financially unstable, but the money that we saved carried us and we continued to tithe from the little income that was coming into our household. In September 2013, a part-time opportunity came through my former principal to assist him in the preparation for a new school that was opening the following school year. That temporary position became permanent and now I'm part of the leadership team.

God operates best in situations where you can't rely on your own power. When you surrender yourself and your circumstances to Him, He has no choice but to make Himself known because that's what He promised. His timing is not like ours; He doesn't own a calendar and He's doesn't care about time zones. Since God is omnipresent, He's always available. So when he calls you to a new level in your worship ministry, don't be afraid! Remember, He's graced you for this assignment. If you need assurance or direction, ask the Giver for strategy and clarity. Rest assured, His plan will not look like anything you've witnessed before in others, and quite frankly, it shouldn't because it's His plan for YOU. Because you're unique, your plan will be unique. When you understand that your assignment is temporary, you realize that transition is inevitable. Obey the voice of our Father and trust Him to direct your path.

Next Level Preparation

1 Samuel 16:4a (NLT)- So Samuel did as the Lord instructed...

In fall 2013, I began playing for a small church in Bartlett, TN. I saw the job posting at The University of Memphis during the Independent Music Teacher's Conference. During my talk with the pastor, I wasn't thrilled about the compensation, but, comparing this assignment to the one I'd just left, I felt that this opportunity would be a better fit for me.

Serving as the musician for this church was a great experience. The worship leader was Spirit-led and the praise team wanted to participate, which made it easy to serve. The biggest blessing that came out of this assignment was the preparation that God was providing to me through the pastor.

In the season of my assignment, the pastor was transitioning out of his full-time job to focus on ministry. He preached often about faith, obedience, and shared his personal testimony as he endured the journey. He and his wife also offered advice to my husband and me during our engagement. We had many discussions with them concerning marriage and dealing with blended families. Pastor's teachings were critical to the next level that God was taking me; I can't imagine where I'd be now had I'd said no to the assignment because of the pay.

As you are serving as a worship leader, know that God is using this assignment to prepare you towards your purpose. Just as God instructed Samuel to obey the first command (1 Samuel 16:1-4), that is what He desires of you at this moment; He will reveal the next step once you've obeyed the first task. It's natural for you to question God; in this passage, Samuel was trying to keep from getting killed by Saul. Will your next assignment be in the field of music or in a church? No one knows but God. Remember that God is the Master Strategist and he promised in His word that you will reap the harvest if you don't quit!

Worship Builders

1 Timothy 4:11-14 (NLT) -Teach these things and insist that everyone learn them. Don't let anyone think less of you because you are young. Be an example to all believers in what you say, in the way you live, in your love, your faith, and your purity. Until I get there, focus on reading the Scriptures to the church, encouraging the believers, and teaching them. Do not neglect the spiritual gift you received through the prophecy spoken over you when the elders of the church laid their hands on you.

As I was transitioning into my new role as a school administrator, God was making it clear that I couldn't teach piano anymore. I asked Him to provide a teacher that I could trust with my students. I cared about my students and refused to leave them without a suitable teacher. Weeks after my prayer, he lead me to a young lady who I sang with in a local community choir. She was soon to graduate with a music education degree and she also had a few private students of her own. After several conversations, I was pleased to hear her desire to learn and I knew that she had the makings of becoming a great teacher.

She began as a "judge", offering advice to my students who were preparing for a keyboard festival. Her advice matched the advice that I would give my students and she also offered new practice ideas and techniques. Later on, I allowed her to co-teach with me, teach lessons in my absence, and finally transferred my students to her once I closed my studio. It felt good being around someone who shared the same passions and values that I had and it was an honor to mentor her.

If God has called you to a specific purpose, He expects you to be available to teach and lead others. Paul saw that Timothy would experience resistance because of his young age. Just because you feel that you may not have enough skill or experience doesn't mean that you can't share what you know. Satan hates growth; don't allow the enemy to distract you with excuses to prevent edification. If you're walking in purpose, you can give freely. There is no insecurity or envy because you understand that God has purposed you for a specific work.

Conclusion: Worship Promotes Change

John 12:32 (KJV) -And I, if I be lifted up from the earth, will draw all men unto me.

Just as worship begins in holy expectancy, it ends in holy obedience. If worship does not propel us into greater obedience, it has not been worship. To stand before the Holy One of eternity is to change. - Richard Foster, from the book Celebration of Discipline

If you were like me, you would get so pumped when the church members would stand up during praise and worship, lift their hands during a song, shout before the pastor presents the sermon, and pat you on the back with words of encouragement after the service was over. You thought, "God, you really used me today. Church was awesome!" On the Sundays where the exact opposite happened, you felt like a failure and begin replaying all the events that occurred in your life the previous week to find out what you'd done wrong that prevented worship from going forth. Oh, and don't let one of the elders or the pastor ask to see you after church was over. That was like walking on death row. The moment I realized God's love wasn't performance-based, that freed me to love Him the way I was created to love Him (John 4:23-24 MSG).

So the question remains, "How do I know if my ministry is fruitful?" The question is easy. Remove the word "my". It's not your ministry; it's God's ministry that He's assigned you to. This is what we call Kingdom work.

Ok, so let's rephrase the question: How do we know that we're effective in the Kingdom? We won't be influential until we're yielded, completely surrendered to God, so others can see Him through us. This means that we must make a personal choice to change who we think we are or should be to who God desires for us to be. When our hearts change, our lives change. Then the hearts and lives of those around us, including our co-laborers in music ministry and the church congregation, will change as well. Mindsets will be renewed! Deliverance and healing will manifest! Discipleship will be a no-brainer!

Are you ready to be a worship builder? I hope that my journey has encouraged you to go forth!

This is my prayer for you…

Father, I thank you for every person that You have called to this assignment. I am assured that they are anointed and appointed for the task at hand. I pray the words that You gave to Joshua over each laborer, to be strong and courageous. . If they're afraid, I pray that they step out afraid knowing that the same resurrection power You gave to Jesus lives inside each and every one of them!

Strengthen them to call on You when they are hurt or confused and not lean to their own understanding. Surround your servants with wise counsel, those who have a heart for leadership and will prepare your servants to be great leaders as well.

I declare that the manifestation of Your kingdom, Father, will be radiant as you move forward in the current season of their lives.

In Jesus' name, Amen.

ABOUT THE AUTHOR

Sonja Jones is a "builder of lives". Before her roles of wife, mother, educator, musician, entrepreneur, and leader, she is lover of God first.

Her mission is to ignite growth in others by being a living testimony of God's goodness. Sonja's love for music has touched hundreds of lives in Memphis, TN throughout her 13-year career as a music educator and church pianist. She currently resides in the Memphis area with her husband, Marreco, and sons, Macarius, Ladarius, Yero, Jireh and Tyler.

For more information on resources and events, visit www.sonjarjones.com.